American History

Who's
Clues? ™

By
Nathan Levy

D1115374

MIND
MOTION™

TREND enterprises, Inc.

Introduction

What better way to provide a fun, change of pace than with a Whose Clues?™ book! Not only do you have fun trying to guess the answer, but also you are developing creative, divergent thinking skills.

Each page gives five clues that describe a famous person or character. By listening to each of the clues, asking questions, and working together, players guess the person's or character's identity. Participants will have many chances to develop cooperative learning and deductive thinking skills—without even realizing it. Whose Clues?™ provides unlimited teaching and learning opportunities that kids from ages 8 to 88 love!

How to Use This Book

1. The object is to identify the person or character described by the clues.

2. Choose a reader to read the first clue. Always read only one clue at a time.

3. Remind the players to listen carefully to the clue. After hearing the clue they may ask "yes" or "no" questions and work together to figure out the answer. Answer their questions only with "yes" or "no" responses. Allow adequate time for the questions.

4. Read the next clue and repeat the process until all the clues have been read, or until someone correctly identifies the person or character.

5. If the players are clearly stuck and frustrated after several repetitions, feel free to give them hints.

Who am I?

- I was a jack-of-all-trades.

- I worked with Adams, Jefferson, and Madison.

- *Poor Richard* shared my ideas about frugality and industry.

- "A penny saved is a penny earned."

- I enjoyed flying kites in the rain.

1

Benjamin Franklin

Who am I?

- I was a seamstress.

- I was tired when I broke the unfair law.

- My feet hurt so I sat down and didn't move.

- Because of my "uncivil" actions, I have the right to sit anywhere on the bus.

- I love to see parks with roses in Montgomery.

Rosa Parks

2

Who am I?

- There was a dark side to my visit having nothing to do with Darth Vader.

- The gravity of my situation was very serious.

- I flew with eagles.

- I took a small step, but wow was it a leap!

- I was the first man on the moon.

3

Neil Armstrong

Who am I?

- I was in the theater.

- I was in the theater (this is not a typographical error).

- I would have hated modern pennies.

- After slavery ended I got my revenge.

- I ended Abraham Lincoln's presidency.

4

Who am I?

- My name meant *playful one.*

- The English thought I was an Indian princess.

- Jamestown, Virginia, was my home before it had a name.

- John Smith owed his life to me.

- Disney made an animated film about my life.

Pocahontas

Who am I?

- I couldn't move around very well.

- I kept my job longer than anyone else ever did or will.

- I made my dog famous in one of my speeches.

- "...a day that will live in infamy," are my words.

- Eleanor was my first lady.

Who am I?

- I was a Quaker.

- Though others chose to wear dresses, I wore bloomers to make a statement.

- My friends and I wanted our voices to be heard and opinions to count.

- My picture was circulated all over the country long after I had died.

- I fought for the right to vote and became prominent on the dollar coin.

7

Susan B. Anthony

Who am I?

- My life began in Harlem in 1937.

- I was the youngest person ever to hold my position.

- The army became my life's calling.

- I earned the respect of the world for my work in the Middle East.

- I was the chairman of the Joint Chiefs of Staff during the Persian Gulf War.

Colin Powell

8

Who am I?

- No one had ever played my position before.

- My co-workers allow me to go first when we are away from the job.

- I gave up my law practice for a better position.

- My colleagues and I make up the equivalent of a baseball team.

- I was the first female Supreme Court Justice.

9 Sandra Day O'Connor

Who am I?

- I was a silversmith in Boston.

- My yelling was important, as were my equestrian skills.

- I believed in repetition.

- People have two legs and two _____. Fill in the blank and you will have a hint.

- The British are coming.

Paul Revere

10

Who am I?

- My father taught me how to find my way through the woods.

- I became famous for my work in transportation.

- I was considered the "Moses of my people."

- Many slaves had me to thank for their freedom.

- I was a leader in the Underground Railroad.

11 Harriet Tubman

Who am I?

- I was the first to visit all 50 states.

- I enjoyed a good debate, and once had one in the kitchen.

- My home in California had a gate and no water to be found.

- Ford became famous, when I resigned from my position.

- I was the first President to resign from office.

Richard Nixon

12

Who am I?

- Overcoming was my game.

- Rosa deserved the same!

- Dreams added to my fame.

- Equality was my aim.

- Royalty was in my name.

Martin Luther King, Jr.

Who am I?

- I was first in 1776.

- George was chosen over me.

- Sam and I escaped after Paul's call.

- I write large.

- "Put your _____ _____ here," is one way to ask people to sign their names. Fill in the blanks and you will have the answer.

John Hancock

14

Who am I?

- I was the first to act in this role.

- I came to the United States as a refugee from Czechoslovakia.

- I set my sights on the world.

- I may be a secretary, but I don't type or file.

- I was the first female Secretary of State.

15

Madeleine Albright

Who am I?

- My hair wasn't real.

- I can give you a clue if you give me a dollar bill.

- I was a general.

- I have a city named after me.

- My presidency was the first.

Who am I?

- I'm known for my diplomacy.

- I was the first President born in a hospital.

- After my presidency, I became a carpenter.

- I love to see peanuts in Plains.

- Georgia is on my mind.

17

Jimmy Carter

Who am I?

- I kept my eyes on the skies.

- The first time I went
  with friends, but I enjoyed
  it so much that I had to try
  it again by myself.

- I became known for
  conquering the Atlantic.

- My last trip is a mystery
  to everyone but me.

- I was a famous female pilot.

Amelia Earhart

18

Who am I?

- I was truly gifted.

- The day of my death is celebrated with fireworks all over the land.

- I was involved in a draft that was one of the most important in the history of America.

- While I was President, I made a large purchase.

- *Jeffersonian* democracy is based on my idea of government.

19

Thomas Jefferson

Who am I?

- I was a famous medicine man.

- I lived most of my life on the Standing Rock Reservation in South Dakota.

- I helped start the Ghost Dance.

- I am often associated with the Battle of the Little Bighorn and Colonel George Custer.

- I was given the name *Tatanka–Iyotanka,* which describes a buffalo bull sitting on its haunches.

Who am I?

- I wore glasses.

- Because of me, you don't have to sail around South America.

- I always believed that you should walk softly and carry a big stick.

- My three friends and I are very prominent in South Dakota.

- The teddy bear got its name from me.

21

Theodore Roosevelt

Who am I?

- Honestly, my nickname was the railsplitter.

- A stovepipe was my signature.

- My address in Gettysburg was memorable.

- Illinois is my land.

- A shot in the dark ended my presidency.

Abraham Lincoln

22

Who am I?

- I spoke out against slavery.

- My name was Isabella.

- The truth is, I changed my name.

- I was a traveling preacher and a sojourner in the eastern United States.

- I became a sojourner, so I could spread the truth about slavery.

Sojourner Truth

Who am I?

- You could say I was good at languages.

- I helped two friends on their rocky expedition through my native land.

- More than 20 monuments and landmarks honor my name.

- Even though I lived long before Susan B. Anthony, she became the first, and I the second on the dollar coin.

- I was an interpreter for Lewis and Clark.

Sacagawea

24

Who am I?

- I was famous for the color schemes I created.

- My work has been flown all over the world.

- My original design became outdated.

- New York, New Jersey, and Virginia were stars in my eyes.

- I sewed Old Glory.

25

Betsy Ross

Who am I?

- Education was important to me.

- I am known for the school I founded.

- I was the Wizard of Tuskegee and considered one of the most influential leaders of my time.

- I share my last name with the first U.S. President.

- My first name sounds like something you might read.

Who am I?

- I wrote a daily newspaper column.

- When my husband had difficulty getting around, I was the first lady to help him.

- I have been called the most influential woman in American politics.

- My uncle and my husband shared a career as well as a name.

- My husband, Franklin, was a leader of the free world.

27 Eleanor Roosevelt

Who am I?

- I was the second of nine children.

- I was the youngest elected to my position.

- My reign is often referred to as Camelot.

- My younger brother and I met the same fate.

- I was the first Roman Catholic to be elected President.

John F. Kennedy 28